Alex Morgan

By Jon M. Fishman

AMAZING ATHLETES

Lerner Publications ◆ Minneapolis

Lerner Publications Company
A division of Lerner Publishing Group, Inc.
241 First Avenue North
Minneapolis, MN 55401 USA

For reading levels and more information, look up this title at www.lernerbooks.com.

Library of Congress Cataloging-in-Publication Data

Fishman, Jon M.
    Alex Morgan / by Jon M. Fishman.
        pages cm. — (Amazing athletes)
    Includes bibliographical references and index.
    ISBN 978-1-4677-9386-5 (lb : alk. paper) — ISBN 978-1-4677-9621-7 (pb : alk. paper) —
ISBN 978-1-4677-9622-4 (eb pdf)
    1. Morgan, Alex (Alexandra Patricia), 1989– —Juvenile literature. 2. Women soccer players—
United States—Biography—Juvenile literature. I. Title.
GV942.7.M673F57 2016
796.334092—dc23 [B]   2015033938

Manufactured in the United States of America
2-41645-20316-3/21/2016

TABLE OF CONTENTS

Colombian player Catalina Perez trips Alex as she goes for a goal in the 2015 World Cup.

ON TOP OF THE WORLD

Alex Morgan sprinted after the bouncing soccer ball. There was nothing but wide-open space between her and the **goalkeeper**. Just as Alex reached the ball, the goalkeeper slid into her. The ball rolled away as Alex slammed into the ground. The **referee** blew the whistle. The goalkeeper was called for a penalty!

Alex and the United States Women's National Team (USWNT) were playing against Colombia on June 22, 2015. It was a World Cup match. The World Cup is the biggest soccer **tournament** in the world.

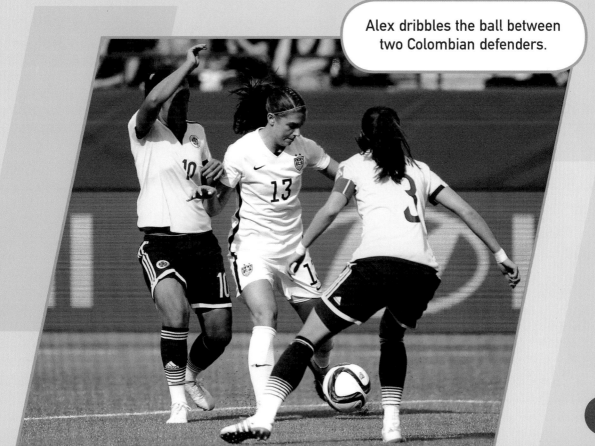

Alex dribbles the ball between two Colombian defenders.

Because the Colombian goalkeeper was called for a penalty for knocking Alex down, the USWNT earned a **penalty kick**. Abby Wambach took the kick, but she missed. The score stayed tied, 0–0. The USWNT had another penalty kick later in the match. This time, Carli Lloyd sent the ball into the goal for a 1–0 lead.

Alex has her mind on her team's next move during the June 2015 match against Colombia.

Alex *(right)* and Colombian player Carolina Arias both go for the ball. The two teams were evenly matched.

Not long before the World Cup began, Alex had injured her knee playing soccer. Instead of practicing with the USWNT, she spent time healing. When the United States played its first World Cup match on June 8, she still wasn't fully healed. But by the time of the Colombia match, she felt strong again. "I feel better and better each game," Alex said.

Alex didn't miss on her second chance at a goal!

Alex showed off her strength later in the match. She raced down the right side of the field with the ball. She spotted Wambach in front of the goal. But just as Alex was about to pass the ball to Wambach, Alex changed her mind. Instead of passing, Alex fired a blast at the net. The goalkeeper got a hand on the ball, but it wasn't enough. The ball bounced into the net for another US goal.

The USWNT won the game, 2–0. Then the team kept on winning. In the championship match, the United States blew Japan off the field. The US women scored five goals and won the game, 5–2. Alex and the USWNT had won the 2015 World Cup!

Teammates Ali Krieger *(left)* and Lauren Holiday *(center)* celebrate with Alex after she scored a goal.

Alex was born in Diamond Bar, California.

SPORTS FAN

On July 2, 1989, Alexandra Patricia Morgan was born in Diamond Bar, California. Diamond Bar is near Los Angeles. Her parents, Mike and Pam, called her Alex. Alex has two older sisters named Jeni and Jeri.

Alex loved to play sports. She tried just about everything. She took part in volleyball, softball, and track and field. One of her favorite sports was **tetherball**. When she was eight years old, Alex decided she wanted to play in the Olympic Games someday. She just didn't know what sport she would play when she got there.

Alex played to win. Whether it was tetherball or a board game, she always wanted to come out on top. She often raced against her sister Jeri. "She would always, always beat me," Alex said. But when Alex was nine years old, she finally beat Jeri. "I was so excited," Alex said.

Alex loved to play video games as a child. Two of her favorites were *Mario Kart* and *Mario Party*.

In 1999, the USWNT won the soccer World Cup. Led by stars such as Mia Hamm and Brandi Chastain, the team was hugely popular in the United States. Alex loved the fast-paced action. And she was thrilled that the USWNT had proven to be the best team in the world. She decided she wanted to play soccer.

The USWNT's big win in 1999 inspired many young girls to play soccer.

Five- and six-year-old girls play soccer with the American Youth Soccer Organization (AYSO).

Alex began playing with the American Youth Soccer Organization (AYSO). The AYSO is open to all kids. Games were at Diamond Bar's Paul C. Grow Park. The AYSO is just for fun, but Alex wanted to win. She tried to control the ball all the time. She would even push other players to get the ball. Alex had a lot to learn about playing on a team.

When she was 14 years old, Alex began playing with Cypress Futbol Club. The soccer organization has boys' and girls' teams for ages eight through 19. Alex's team played against top teams in the area. Players were more skilled than they had been in the AYSO. "Just coming from AYSO, I didn't really know what to expect," said Alex's dad, Mike. But right away, Alex had no trouble keeping up with her teammates. Mike realized his daughter had a chance to be a special soccer player.

Alex's senior picture from the Diamond Bar High School yearbook

MOVING UP, MOVING ON

When she wasn't playing for Cypress, Alex was a star on the Diamond Bar High School girls' soccer team. She became known for her speed and strength near the goal. Diamond Bar soccer coach Kemp Wells liked what he saw in Alex. She had the talent to score goals, and she worked hard to get better.

Alex practices her dribbling skills. Long before she turned pro, she had the determination to excel at soccer.

By the time she was a high school senior, Alex was known as one of the top young players in the country. Coaches chose her for the Under-20 (U-20) Women's National Team. It was a big honor for the 17-year-old. But during practice with the team, Alex was **tackled** from behind. She fell and injured a **ligament** in her knee. Alex needed surgery.

The time away from soccer was a test for Alex. It was hard for her to be off the field for so long, and many young athletes might have given up on their dreams after suffering such a setback. But Alex wanted to play soccer in college. And from the time she was eight years old, she had dreamed of playing in the Olympics.

Alex went to **rehab** three or four times a week. She pushed herself to return to the soccer field as quickly as possible. After about five months, she was back. It was a fast recovery for her type of injury.

Alex's nickname is Baby Horse. Teammates call her that because she is such a fast and powerful runner—just like a horse!

With her knee injury behind her, it was time for the next stage of Alex's soccer career. In 2007, she started school at the University of California, Berkeley (Cal). Even though she was only a first-year student, she quickly became the team's best scorer. She knocked in eight goals her first season, the most on the team. She also pitched in with plenty of **assists**. Alex had learned to be a team player.

Alex *(right)* outruns a North Korean player during the U-20 World Cup final in 2008.

FIRST WORLD TITLE

In addition to playing for Cal, Alex was still a member of the U-20 national team. In 2008, the team played in the U-20 World Cup in Chile. Alex and her teammates made it all the way to the championship game. They faced North Korea for the U-20 World Cup title.

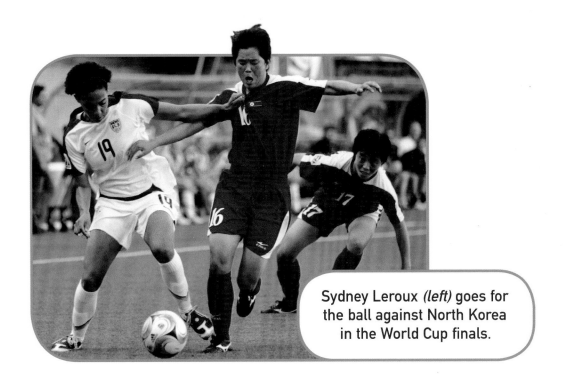

Sydney Leroux *(left)* goes for the ball against North Korea in the World Cup finals.

The championship game against North Korea was a tough battle. The North Koreans were all over the field, making it hard for the US team to hold onto the ball. At 23 minutes into the game, Alex fired a shot at the goal. It bounced away, but a teammate collected the ball and passed it to Sydney Leroux. With a quick turn, Leroux fired the ball into the net for a goal. Team USA took the lead, 1–0.

About 20 minutes later, Alex took a bouncing pass near the **sideline**. She sprinted away from a **defender**. She hung onto the ball as she rushed past two more North Korean players. Then Alex darted to her left. She fired a shot as she fell backward. The ball rocketed into the upper-left corner of the net. Goal!

Alex *(left)* celebrates her goal with her teammates on the sidelines.

An excited US team celebrates after defeating North Korea in the 2008 U-20 World Cup.

North Korea scored late in the game to make the score 2–1. They attacked with everything they had, but they couldn't score again. Alex's goal was enough for the victory. The United States was the U-20 World Cup champion!

Back at Cal, Alex kept putting the ball in the goal. She was on pace to become the school's all-time scoring leader. But her role with the national team often took her away from college. In 2010, she helped Team USA **qualify** for the upcoming World Cup.

Alex wrote a series of children's books called The Kicks. The books are about a middle school soccer team in California.

When Alex graduated from Cal later that year, she had scored 45 goals for the school. That was the third most in the school's history.

Alex scores one for Cal against the Washington State Cougars in 2010.

Alex outruns an opponent during the 2011 World Cup game against France.

DREAM COME TRUE

At the World Cup in 2011, the USWNT made it to the **semifinal** round. If they could beat France, they would play in the championship match. With the score tied 1–1 late in the game, Abby Wambach scored for the United States. The French fought hard to score again.

About three minutes after the Wambach goal, France moved the ball near the front of the US net. USWNT players moved in. The ball popped out to Megan Rapinoe. The US **midfielder** launched the ball to the other end of the field. Alex was the only US player in the area. She sprinted past a French defender and launched the ball. It flew into the net for a goal! The USWNT beat France, 3–1. But the US women lost the championship game to Japan.

Alex celebrates after scoring against France.

In 2012, the Summer Olympic Games were held in London, England. The USWNT would need Alex's big-time scoring punch to win the gold medal. The team faced Canada in the semifinal round in what turned out to be a historic game.

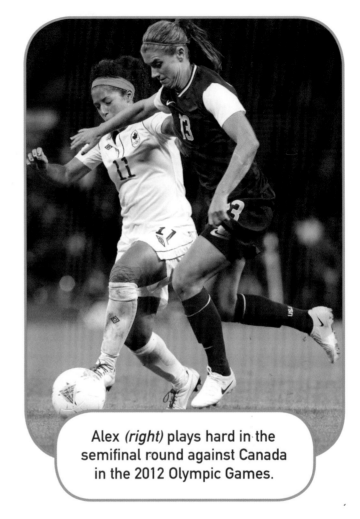

Alex *(right)* plays hard in the semifinal round against Canada in the 2012 Olympic Games.

The two teams were evenly matched. Canada scored first. Then the United States tied the game, 1–1. Canada scored again. The USWNT

Alex *(left)* and Saki Kumagai of Japan fight for possession of the ball during the final match of the 2012 Olympic Games.

knocked one in to make the score 2–2. One more goal by each team made the score 3–3.

The game went to **extra time**. With the clock ticking away, Heather O'Reilly of the United States sent a high pass to the front of the Canadian goal. Alex soared and smacked the ball with her head. The ball slipped in for the game-winning goal! Three days later, the USWNT beat Japan for the gold medal.

A happy Alex kisses her Olympic gold medal.

Alex had fulfilled her childhood dream of playing in the Olympics. And not only that—she had helped her team take home the gold. "I had one dream when I was eight years old, and I was able to accomplish that dream," she said. "That's possible with believing in yourself." Alex will keep on believing in herself, and she'll continue to make her dreams a reality on the soccer field.

Selected Career Highlights

2015   Helped the USWNT win the World Cup

2014   Began playing with the Portland Thorns FC

2012   Helped the USWNT win a gold medal at the Olympic Games

2011   Chosen by the Western New York Flash with the first overall pick in the Women's Professional Soccer draft
Helped the USWNT make it to the World Cup final

2010   Led Cal with 14 goals
Graduated from Cal

2009   Led Cal with 14 goals

2008   Helped the US win the U-20 World Cup
Led Cal with nine goals

2007   Began attending school at Cal
Led Cal with eight goals

2006   Chosen to play for the U-20 Women's National Team
Injured a ligament in her knee

2003   Began playing soccer with Cypress Futbol Club

1999   Decided that she wanted to be a soccer player

1997   Decided that she wanted to be in the Olympics someday

Glossary

assists: passes to teammates that help score goals

defender: a soccer player who plays a defensive position

extra time: time added to the end of a soccer match if the score is tied

goalkeeper: a player who defends the goal

ligament: a tough band that connects bones

midfielder: a player who usually runs in the middle of the field

penalty kick: a free kick at the goal

qualify: to win enough games to be included in a tournament

referee: a person who watches a match to make sure players are following the rules

rehab: an exercise program used to heal injuries

semifinal: the next-to-last game in a tournament

sideline: the edge of a soccer field

tackled: blocked or kicked when in possession of the ball

tetherball: a game with a ball attached by a rope to the top of a pole. Players strike the ball and try to wrap the rope around the pole.

tournament: a set of games held to decide the best team

Further Reading & Websites

Eason, Sarah, and Paul Mason. *Street Soccer*. Minneapolis: Lerner Publications, 2012.

Fishman, Jon M. *Abby Wambach*. Minneapolis: Lerner Publications, 2014.

Fishman, Jon M. *Carli Lloyd*. Minneapolis: Lerner Publications, 2016.

Alex Morgan's Official Website
http://www.alexmorgansoccer.com
This website has photos and videos about Alex, information about soccer camps, and much more.

Sports Illustrated Kids
http://www.sikids.com
The *Sports Illustrated Kids* website covers all sports, including soccer.

US Women's National Team
http://www.ussoccer.com/womens-national-team
The official website of the USWNT is chock-full of content about the World Cup champions.

Expand learning beyond the printed book. Download free, complementary educational resources for this book from our website, www.lerneresource.com.

Index

Photo Acknowledgments

The images in this book are used with the permission of: © Todd Korol/
Getty Images, pp. 4, 8; © Kevin C. Cox/Getty Images, p. 5; © Maddie Meyer/
FIFA/Getty Images, pp. 6, 9; ©Geoff Robins/AFP/Getty Images, p. 7; © Irfan
Kahn/Los Angeles Times/Getty Images, p. 10; AP Photo/Michael Caufield,
p. 12; © Al Schaben/Los Angeles Times/Getty Images, p. 13; Seth Poppel
Yearbook Library, pp. 15, 16; AP Photo/Santiago Llanquin, pp. 19, 20, 22;
AP Photo/Roberto Candia, p. 21; © Collegiate Images/Getty Images, p. 23;
© Mike Hewitt/FIFA/Getty Images, p. 24; © Boris Streubel/Getty Images,
p. 25; © Stanley Chou/Getty Images, p. 26; © Stuart Franklin/FIFA/Getty
Images, pp. 27, 29; © Jamie Squire/Getty Images, p. 28.

Front cover: © Rich Lam/Getty Images.

Main body text set in Caecilia LT Std 55 Roman 16/28.
Typeface provided by Adobe Systems.